iVY+BEAN+ME

A FILL-IN-THE-BLANK BOOK

written by annie barrows + illustrated by sophie blackall

chronicle books · san francisco

Hi Out There!

Our teacher, Ms. Aruba-Tate, is really nice, but she has some wacko ideas. One of her ideas was that we should write in a journal every day. Every day! We were supposed to write a whole page! Who has a whole page of things happen to them every day? No one! For a long time, we just wrote really big. But then we got a better idea: we decided to make up questions and answer them, which is a lot easier and more interesting, too. We thought up some great questions! (Which do you like better, spit or earwax?)

And then we thought up some
   great answers! We also wrote
   down some extra ideas for not
   being bored.
    We decided that other
kids might like to answer our
questions, so we put them in this
book. We included a few of our
answers, but not all of them. We
wanted to leave you guys plenty
of room for your own answers and
drawings and ideas.

   Have fun!

Ivy + Bean
(earwax)   (spit)

My name is

_____

_____

I wish my name were

_____

_____

My birthday is

(Circle the month and the day.)

Jan	July	1	2	3	4	5	6
Feb	Aug	7	8	9	10	11	12
Mar	Sept	13	14	15	16	17	18
Apr	Oct	19	20	21	22	23	24
May	Nov	25	26	27	28	29	
June	Dec	30	31				

Year _____

My family has _____ people in it.
They are

_____

_____

_____

_____

_____

_____

_____

_____

My sister
Nancy looks
like this!

_____

_____

_____

_____

_____

They look like this

My friend's name is _____
She (or he) (or it!) looks like this

And then my other friends are

We have a
friend named
Prairie!

My other friends look like this

My imaginary friends are named

They look like this

I have friends that no one else can see, but they're not imaginary. One is named Ociceo, but I can't tell you the other's name. It's secret.

My best friend to have a secret with is

_____

_____

My best friend to make potions with is

_____

_____

_____

Ivy!
Duh!

My best friend to dig for buried treasure with is

Bean! Duh!

_____

Amazing People

Who can hold her breath the longest?

_____

Vanessa's little brother Toby can hold his breath for 76 seconds!

Who can do a backbend?

_____

_____

_____

_____

ZUZU!

Who can burp on purpose?

_____

_____

Dusit can burp the whole alphabet.

It's gross.

Who laughs the most?

_____

I am.

Who is the bravest?

_____

Yeah.
You are.

The wackiest thing
I ever did was

_____

_____

_____

_____

_____

_____

_____

_____

_____

_____

I would do it again.

☐ Yes   ☐ No

I live in

- ☐ a house
- ☐ an apartment
- ☐ a tent
- ☐ a bus
- ☐ a tree house
- ☐ a cave
- ☐ a castle
- ☐ a submarine
- ☐ a yurt
- ☐ something else that isn't on this list

Here's what it looks like

Here's what it looks like.

Here's what my neighborhood looks like

If I could live anyplace,
I'd like to live in

I'd live in
a tree.

My favorite thing about my room is

If I could have anything I wanted,
my room would look like this

I would paint the walls this color

(Fill in the box with the color you want.)

My bed would be made out of

_____

_____

_____

_____

I'd sleep in a giant shell hung from the ceiling on silver threads, so it would rock back and forth.

I'd sleep in a hammock, like pirates do.

There would be a secret password to get into my room and it would be

_____

_____

_____

_____

Secret.

(Cover this up with a paper flap so no one can see it!)

I wouldn't have a password. I'd have a moat.

My favorite color is

(Fill in the box with the color.)

My favorite day of the week is

(Circle the day.)

Mon   Tue   Wed   Thu   Fri   Sat   Sun

Thursday.

Why?

I don't know.
I just said that.

My favorite time is

12:34

My favorite holiday is

_____

_____

My favorite season is _____

_____

Summer!

My favorite ice-cream flavor is

_____

My favorite kind of cake is

_____

I hope my next birthday cake
looks like this

Things I collect are

The thing I would most like to find is

A magic wand.

A dirt bike.

List of books I like

List of books I don't like

_____

_____

_____

_____

_____

_____

_____

_____

The animal I would most like to be is

_____

_____

The animal I would most like to have as a pet is

_____

_____

I wish I had a tiny monkey.

What I really want is a sloth, but a kitten would be nice, too.

The animal I do have as a pet is

_____

My pet's name is_____
It looks like this

List of good pet names

Ugthorpe,
Bolivia,
Fruit Cup.

You are
so weird.

List of good kid names

I know a kid named Toad.

That's pretty good.

If I could have three wishes come true, they would be

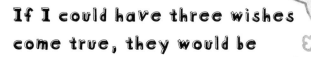

1. _____

_____

_____

2. _____

_____

_____

3. _____

_____

_____

If I had to pick one age
to be forever, I would be

SEVEN!

If I were going to get
one superpower, it would be

Flying, for sure.

What about
shape-shifting?
Then you could fly
if you wanted to.

You're right.
Shape-shifting.

Things that give me the creeps are

_____

_____

_____

_____

_____

_____

_____

_____

_____

_____

_____

_____

_____

My worst enemy is _____

_____

because _____

_____

_____

_____

_____

_____

_____

_____

_____

Mrs. Trantz.
She's so mean.

I'm not sure.
Mrs. Trantz is pretty
bad, but at least she
can't run very fast.

Would You Rather . . . ?

(Circle your choice.)

Eat an **ant** or a **feather**

Lots of people eat ants.

Eat a **snail** or step in **dog poop**

Snail!

Dog poop!

Go **shopping** for ladies'
clothes for three hours
or
go to a **wedding** where
you were the only kid

Eat **lima beans** or
raw **cauliflower**

Would You Rather . . . ?

(Circle your choice.)

Break your **arm** or your **leg**

Be eaten by a **shark** or a **lion**

Be able to **fly**
or **breathe underwater**

Be a **fairy** or a **witch**

. . . **witch** or **mermaid**

. . . **mermaid** or **unicorn**

. . . **unicorn** or **dragon**

If I could make one magic potion that would really work, it would be

_____

_____

_____

_____

_____

_____

_____

_____

INVISIBILITY SPELL

INGREDIENTS

PREPARATIO

I want a potion to make me invisible. Then I can play tricks on people and they won't know who did it. And then I'll laugh really hard.

My list of potion ingredients

1. _____

2. _____

3. _____

4. _____

5. _____

6. _____

7. _____

8. _____

9. _____

10. _____

Right now, I've got sap, dried apples, dead flies, wax, nutmeg, baking soda, dead spiders, pine needles, yellow stuff that my mom gave me, and some Barbie hair.

My favorite dinosaur is

The world record
I'd like to break is

_____

_____

_____

The world record I might
really break is

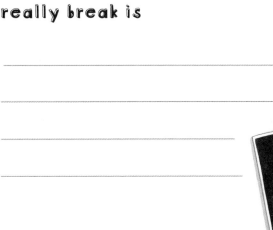

_____

_____

_____

_____

My favorite babysitter is

_____

because _____

_____

_____

_____

_____

_____

_____

_____

_____

_____

Leona, because she can draw perfect horses.

The thing that the babysitter lets me do that my parents don't is

_____

_____

_____

_____

_____

_____

_____

Leona lets me make my own snacks.

The latest I ever stayed up was

because

The nicest thing I ever did was

The most trouble I ever got into was

_____

_____

_____

_____

_____

_____

_____

A really bad word I would never say is

(Write it in the box and then erase it!)

**When I get in trouble,
my grown-ups take away**

☐ Dessert

☐ TV

☐ My computer

☐ My favorite toys

☐ They don't take things away,

but I have to stay in my room

☐ Other

All of the above.
Sheesh.

Something that was less fun
than I expected was

_____

_____

_____

_____

_____

_____

_____

_____

Something that was more fun
than I expected was

If I had to be in a ballet, I'd like
my costume to look like this

List of things I do to help stop climate change

_____

_____

_____

_____

_____

_____

_____

_____

_____

_____

_____

_____

The most money I ever
found on the sidewalk was

If I had $10, I'd spend it on

_____

_____

_____

_____

A doll coffin.

_____

If I had $20, I'd spend it on

_____

_____

_____

A leaf blower.

_____

_____

If I ran a camp, it would be called

_____

_____

Camp Flaming Arrow!

Camp Neanderthal Flaming Arrow!

At my camp the rules would be

_____

_____

_____

_____

_____

_____

At my camp the activities would be

_____

_____

_____

_____

_____

_____

_____

_____

_____

_____

_____

_____

_____

List of crafts I like

List of crafts I think are dumb

Anything where you have to be really careful.

My favorite movie is

_____

_____

If I were a spy, my code name would be

_____

_____

_____

My list of spying tips

You understand people a lot better if you look in their windows.

Three mysterious things that have happened to me are

1. _____

_____

_____

_____

2. _____

_____

_____

_____

3. _____

_____

_____

_____

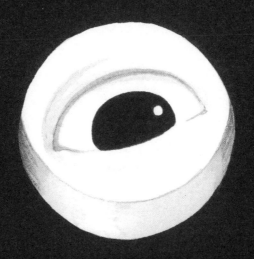

I have seen a ghost

☐ yes   ☐ no

. . . and it looked like this

There was a ghost
in the bathroom
at our school!

If I wanted to hide a diamond, I'd put it

_____

_____

_____

_____

_____

There's a secret place that nobody knows about but me, and it's

(Cover this up with a paper flap so no one can see it!)

_____

_____

_____

_____

_____

_____

A really great
April Fools' Trick is

_____

_____

_____

_____

_____

_____

_____

One time I took the pillows out
of my dad's pillowcases and put
balloons in there instead. When
he went to bed, he yelled.

The last time I laughed really really hard was when

When my
dad yelled.

Something I did that was probably not a good idea

_____

_____

_____

_____

_____

Something I did that was a good idea

_____

_____

_____

_____

Something I did that other people copycatted

_____

_____

_____

_____

_____

_____

_____

_____

_____

_____

Presents I'd like to get that
I might really get

Presents I'd like to get that I probably won't get

A doll coffin.

Dirt!

_____

_____

_____

_____

_____

_____

Presents I'd like to get that I definitely won't get

_____

_____

_____

_____

_____

The last time I was really really surprised was when

Design your own backpack

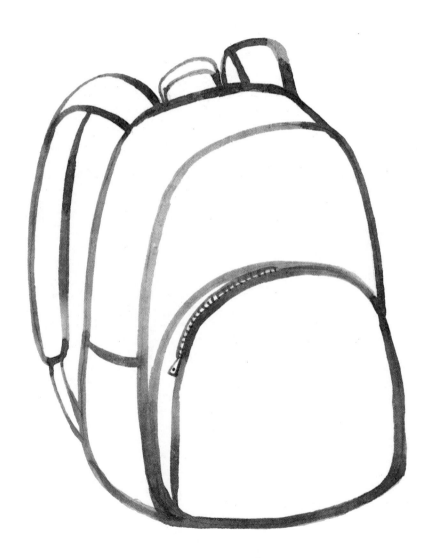

I am in _____ grade,

Our teacher is
Ms. Aruba-Tate!

and my teacher is _____

One time in school we

_____

_____

_____

_____

_____

_____

_____

_____

_____

_____

_____

_____

_____ and everyone laughed.

My favorite grown-up at school is

_____

Ms. Aruba-Tate!

The scariest grown-up at school is

_____

_____

_____

_____

Rose the Yard Duty!

My favorite letter of the alphabet is

(Write it in the box.)

G.

Why?

It just is.

My favorite subject in school is

_____

My favorite PE activity is

Komodo Hunt.

_____

I also like to play

_____
_____
_____

_____

_____

_____

_____

_____

_____

_____

The best field trip we ever went on was

Ways school could be better are

_____

_____

_____

_____

_____

_____

_____

_____

_____

_____

_____

_____

_____

_____

Fun Things You Can Do So You Won't Be Bored

Make-It-Yourself Mystery:

Move the stuff in your house around. Switch the photos on the wall around; put the books in different places; put the living room cushions on different chairs. See how long it takes your family to notice.

Straightjacket:

In this game, you have to walk
in a straight line until you
actually bump into something;
then you can turn.
Try to walk home
from school or your
friend's house this way.

We do this all
the time!

Buried Treasure:

Bury something good, but not too good, in the yard. Then make a treasure map of the spot and tape it to the back of the toilet in your house for the kids who will live there in the future to find.

I buried some tweezers. I dug them up later, though.

Think Like a Carrot:

Spend five minutes trying to make yourself look like a particular vegetable. No costume or makeup required—just try to bend yourself into the shape of a veggie. Think hard about being that vegetable. Make your grown-up guess which vegetable you are.

Hot Lava

Pretend the floor of
your house is hot
lava and try to
get across
the house

without touching it. You can stick pillows
and books to step on in difficult spots,
but you get extra credit if you use fewer
than ten. Don't walk on the tables or the
counters (but skootch across them on your
tush if you can). If you have something you
can roll on, like for instance a big ball or a
skateboard, that's really good.

Measure Stuff

If you have a tape measure (you know, one of those cloth or plastic things with inches and centimeters on it), you can measure anything. It's fun to measure yourself. Did you know that the size of someone's neck is usually twice the size of that person's wrist? And twice the size of the neck usually equals the size of the waist? Crazy, but true!

Do you know that before they're five, kids can't reach over the top of their heads to touch their ears?

That's nuts! Why not?

Their heads are too big, and their arms are too little.

Long Live the Queen!

Someday you may meet a Queen (or a King), and you have to know how to behave.

#1. You have to curtsy when you meet the Queen. To practice curtsying, put one foot in front of the other (doesn't matter which); grab a little hunk of your clothes in each hand, lift it a tiny bit; tilt the top of you toward the Queen; and dip your knees a little. Don't fall over.

#2. You cannot turn your back on the Queen, so you have to know how to leave a room by walking backward without smashing into anything, which is also not allowed. Practice a lot.

#3. You cannot sneeze in front of the Queen. One way to not sneeze is to press hard on either side of your face. The Queen won't mind that at all.

Write with Your Toes

Why? Because your toes are just sitting there, doing nothing. Stick a pencil in between them, and try to write your name.

Go ahead! Use your toes to write something here

Sneaky

Practice walking without making any noise. If you succeed, you will be able to sneak up on people!

You will be able to get really close to squirrels!

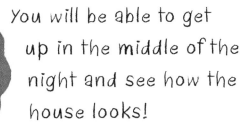

You will be able to get up in the middle of the night and see how the house looks!

Write Your Own
Ivy and Bean Story

Here are the beginnings of some Ivy and Bean stories.
Finish them yourself.

(Write a title here.)

1. _____

Ivy closed her book and sighed. "We don't know how to make anything," she said.

"What do you mean?" yelped Bean. "I can make potholders!"

"I mean we don't know how to make cheese. Or soup. Or anything. We'd never survive on the prairie."

"I know how to make cereal," said Bean.

"They don't have cereal on the prairie," Ivy said. "They have soup."

"Fine," said Bean. "Let's make soup."

2.

Bean's mom said she would buy Bean a book. Any book Bean wanted. At the store, Bean found a really cool sushi pencil-topper. "A book," said Bean's mom. Bean found a set of bug stickers. "A book!" said Bean's mom. Bean found a kit for making your own tattoos. "A BOOK!" said Bean's mom. So Bean found a book called *Sing, Sing, Sing— in Hawaiian!* What a great book!

"You wanna play?" Bean hollered into Ivy's mail slot.

It took Ivy a moment to open the door, and when she did, she was wearing curtains.

Bean looked at her. "Why are you wearing that?"

"I think I'm becoming a mind-reader," Ivy whispered.

"You are?" Bean whispered back. "How do you know?"

"When the phone rang this morning, I knew it was Grandma," Ivy explained. "And it *was.*" She smiled mysteriously.

"Okay, what am I thinking about right—
now!" Bean yelled.

"Elephants," said Ivy.

And you know what? Bean *was* thinking
about elephants! A long line of elephants,
shaking their heads from side to side.

"Wow," Bean said. "That's amazing."

Ivy nodded. "I know. And it just came
over me this morning." Suddenly, she froze.
"Shh!" she whispered, looking toward the
door. "There's someone out there, thinking.
I can hear it!"

Are there any questions we forgot?

Write them down! Then answer them!

Q: _____

_____

A: _____

_____

Q: _____

_____

A: _____

_____

Q: _____

_____

A: _____

_____

_____

Q: _____

_____

A: _____

_____

Q: _____

_____

A: _____

_____

Q: _____

_____

A: _____

_____

_____

Any more thoughts?

Quick, write them down before you forget!

YOU DID IT!

You wrote an
entire book.

You're an author!

Practice your autograph here

_____

Text copyright © 2014 by Annie Barrows.
Illustrations copyright © 2014 by Sophie Blackall.
All rights reserved. No part of this book may be reproduced in any form
without written permission from the publisher.

Manufactured by Leo Paper Products, Heshan, China, in June 2019.

MIX
Paper from
responsible sources
FSC® C020056

FSC
www.fsc.org

Boxed set ISBN 978-1-4521-8453-1
Original hardcover edition ISBN 978-1-4521-3729-2

Design by Kayla Ferriera.
Typeset in Blockhead and Candida.
The illustrations in this book were rendered in Chinese ink.

10 9 8 7 6 5 4 3 2 1

Chronicle Books LLC
680 Second Street
San Francisco, CA 94107

Chronicle Books—we see things differently.
Become part of our community at www.chroniclekids.com.